Popular Teaching Resources

Canadian Character Education

Grades 5-6

Janet Bartier • William Young

Printed in China

Contents

Guidelines for Use

This resource book contains two sections:

- Core Units
- Project Ideas

Each **Core Unit** is made up of a lesson and follow-up worksheets. You will see that in all of the units, "Name", "Date", and the unit topic appear on each follow-up worksheet, so that each one can stand on its own. There is more than one way to present each unit in the book. Here are two that may work for you: (1) give your students the lesson and the worksheets at the same time and let them work on both simultaneously; (2) give just the lesson one day and ask your students to underline key words and ideas or take notes as you talk about the subject, and then give them a worksheet the next day as a quiz.

The **Project Ideas** give students the opportunity to do independent research and then share it with the rest of the class. You may want to adapt them to be up to date with current events.

Happy teaching!

Canadian Character Education

Grades **5-6**

Core Units

Honesty

When talking about honesty, most people think of not telling lies. However, honesty is a lot more than this.

Telling lies is not the only way to be dishonest.

Exaggerating the truth is a sort of lie...

...just as withholding information can be untruthful, too.

While there are many ways to be dishonest, there are also many ways to be honest. Honesty is telling the truth, taking only what is ours, and being fair. It is being truthful in all areas of our lives.

Name: Date:

Honesty

Cut out the words related to honesty. Then paste them to the "Tower of Honesty".

Sincerity
Truth
Self-Discipline
Respect
Selfishness
Openness
Courage
Cruelty
Confidence
Optimism
Friendship

Name: Date:

Honesty

Read what Raymond says. Complete the sentences to explain what the advantages of being honest are. Then write two other advantages on the lines.

lie	peace
trouble	trust

Advantages of Being Honest

- Other people ______________ me.
- I don't have to worry about being caught in a ______________ .
- I am at ______________ with myself.
- I won't be in as much ______________ if I'm honest about something I've done wrong than if I lie about it.
- ____

  ____
- ____

  ____

Name: Date:

Honesty

Read the story. Then answer the questions.

Jamie is always the best student in his class. Last week, Jamie's parents promised to buy him a bike if he got a good mark on his next math quiz. Finally, the quiz came. Jamie was confident that he would soon have a new bike.

Unfortunately, Jamie got only 55% on this math quiz. He was sad and disappointed. On his way home, he kept thinking of the new bike. When he got home, he came up with the idea of changing his wrong answers into correct ones. He knew that his math teacher, Mrs. Beth, might not be aware of the changes because he was usually good at math. As a result, he would have a quiz with a high mark to show his parents and would get his reward.

1. Do you think Jamie's plan will work? Why or why not?

____

____

2. How do you think Mrs. Beth would feel if she found out about Jamie's plan?

____

____

3. How do you think Jamie's parents would feel if they found out how Jamie got the high mark on his math quiz?

____

____

Name: Date:

Honesty

Examine your own words and actions. In your one-week log, write one honest and one dishonest events that happened each day.

SUN	Date:	**Honest:** **Dishonest:**
MON	Date:	**Honest:** **Dishonest:**
TUE	Date:	**Honest:** **Dishonest:**
WED	Date:	**Honest:** **Dishonest:**
THU	Date:	**Honest:** **Dishonest:**
FRI	Date:	**Honest:** **Dishonest:**
SAT	Date:	**Honest:** **Dishonest:**

Name: Date:

Honesty

Look at the picture. Answer the questions.

1. Should George be honest and tell Sue that he broke her doll? Explain.

2. Do you think George needs courage to be honest?

3. Why does it sometimes take courage to be honest?

4. Is there ever a time when we shouldn't be honest? Why or why not?

Name: Date:

Generosity

Generosity is the willingness to give without the expectation of anything in return. It is doing something nice for others without needing others to know it. It is not a sense of obligation, but a sincere passion to do good for others.

Being generous begins with knowing the needs and feelings of others. It is the desire to do what we can to make others' lives happier or easier.

Generosity is not just about giving money. We can be generous:

With Compliments

Little words from the heart, like "You did a great job!" and "Nice try!", or just an encouraging smile can mean a lot to someone.

With Our Time

Doing volunteer work after school or on the weekend is a great way to help others in need.

With Things

This could be as simple as sharing a bag of chips with our friends or donating our used toys to charity.

Name: Date:

Generosity

Keep a log of your generosity. Record what you give, in words or things, to others in a day. You can write or draw to complete the log.

My Giving Log

Date: ____________

I gave ______________________ to ____________ .

Pictures of the things that I gave:

Do you think you were more generous today than other days? Why?

Name: Date:

Generosity

Write a "Thank You" note to someone who has been generous to you. Be sure to say why you are thankful. Add your own design. Then cut it out and send it.

It is important to acknowledge a generous act from others. Sometimes a verbal "thanks" is good enough, but other times it is better to write a "Thank You" note.

THANK YOU

Name: Date:

Generosity

Write about your experiences and feelings.

The Most Generous Thing I've Done:

My Feelings:

The Most Generous Thing Someone Has Done for Me:

My Feelings:

Name: Date:

Generosity

Fill out the coupons and give them as gifts to someone you know on special occasions or at any time.

To: ____________________

From: ____________________

This coupon is good for ____________________

____

To: ____________________

From: ____________________

This coupon is good for ____________________

____

COUPON

To: ____________________

It is good for ____________________

____

From: ____________________

COUPON

To: ____________________

It is good for ____________________

____

From: ____________________

Name: Date:

Generosity

Read the quotation. Then answer the questions.

"That's what I consider true generosity. You give your all, and yet you always feel as if it costs you nothing."

– Simone de Beauvoir

1. Give one example to show how "You give your all, and yet you always feel as if it costs you nothing."

2. Is it hard to give time or care to people in need? Explain.

3. Think of two ways you can give time or charity to people in need, even if you find it hard to do so.

Name: Date:

Respect

Respect is shown in the way we treat other people. When we respect people, we treat them well. When people respect us, they treat us well. Everyone wants to be treated with respect, and that is what we should offer to others.

Being polite to others is one of the basic ways to show respect, but this is not the only thing we do to show respect. There are different ways to show respect to different people.

Following rules, doing our chores, and taking good care of ourselves are some ways we show respect to our parents. We show our friends respect by caring about their feelings, being good listeners, and not talking about them behind their backs. These are also the things we would expect from our friends. Friendships, after all, are built on mutual respect.

Respect given is usually returned. If we respect others, others will respect us. For example, when we respect our teachers and coaches, we gain their respect as interested and active learners.

Name: Date:

Respect

Answer the questions.

Think of a place that you frequent – the library, the community centre, or the movie theatre.

Place: ____________________

1. What do people there do that makes you feel respected?

____

____

2. What do you do there to show respect to others?

____

____

3. Have you done anything there that made someone feel that they were not respected?

____

____

4. Have you experienced any incident there that made you feel disrespected? How did you react?

____

____

Name: Date:

Respect

Give a respectful response to each of the following situations. Explain why you would act that way.

Scenario 1

You are unwrapping a piece of gum and the foil wrapper falls on the ground.

Scenario 2

You are in a hurry, but there are three people ahead of you, blocking your way.

Scenario 3

Your friend wants you to go skiing with her, but you should finish your homework.

Name: Date:

Respect

Write how you show respect and how you could be more respectful.

Family Members

Showing respect: ____________________

Be more respectful: ____________________

Teachers/Coaches

Showing respect: ____________________

Be more respectful: ____________________

Friends

Showing respect: ____________________

Be more respectful: ____________________

Others

Showing respect: ____________________

Be more respectful: ____________________

Name: Date:

Respect

Read what Jason says. Then write some of your favourite ways to show respect.

There are many ways to show respect to others. The key to showing someone respect is to let the person you are interacting with feel that they are valuable. Read three ways that you can act respectfully.

1. **Keep your promise.**

   By keeping your word to others, you not only establish yourself as a person of integrity, but also make other people feel that you value them.

2. **Be on time.**

   Another way to show that you value others is by valuing their time as though it is valuable. Nothing shows this better than being punctual.

3. **Have manners.**

   Try not to interrupt a conversation; be polite; and be generous with "please" and "thank you". By being polite with others, you make them feel valued.

My Favourite Ways to Show Respect

Name: Date:

Respect

Read the quotation. Then answer the questions.

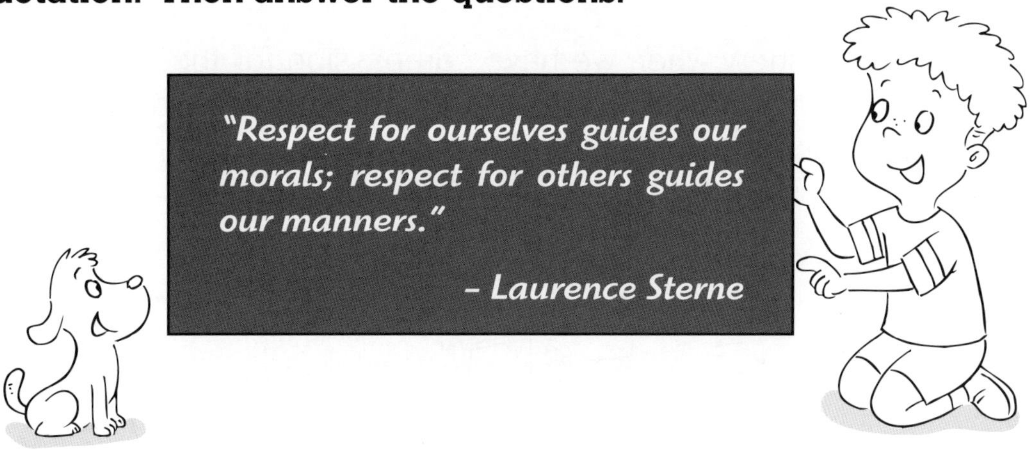

1. Give one example each to show how self-respect guides our morals and how respecting others guides our manners.

____

____

____

____

____

____

2. Write three ways you act at school that show self-respect.

____

____

____

____

____

____

Name: Date:

Charity

Charity is something we show when we have compassion for those in need. We do not have to look far to see where there is need. Animal shelters, food banks, and homeless shelters are all organizations that exist to address needs. They are charitable organizations, and the people that give their time or money to them are showing charity.

Things to Do for Charitable Organizations in Our Community:

- volunteer
- raise funds
- donate money
- raise awareness
- donate goods

Giving to charity is something we do without expecting anything in return. But knowing we have done something to help those who need it is an enormous reward in itself. Try it!

Name: Date:

Charity

The first step to charity is to identify the charitable organizations in your community. Write the names of these organizations in your community, if any, on the lines.

Charitable Organization in My Community

Hospital ____________________

Homeless Shelter ____________________

Seniors' Centre ____________________

Food Bank ____________________

Women's Shelter ____________________

Animal Shelter ____________________

Soup Kitchen ____________________

Others ____________________

Name: Date:

Charity

Look at the words related to charity below. Give an example for each. It can be your own experience or the experience of someone you know.

philanthropist (one who helps those in need)

____

____

____

volunteer

____

____

____

donation

____

____

____

compassion

____

____

____

Name: Date:

Charity

Complete the following and start giving to charity.

Many people give a percentage of their income to charity every month. No matter how little you have to give, it will be appreciated by the charity you donate to.

Four Steps to Donating:

Step 1 My monthly income in total:

Gift money: $ ________

Allowance: $ ________

Others: $ ________

Total: **$ ________**

Step 2 Decide the percentage of income to be donated to charity:

Circle your choice: 5% / 10% / 15% / ________ %

Step 3 Amount I will donate to charity (total income x percentage):

$ ________ X ________ % = $ ________

Step 4 Decide which charities will receive your donation and how much each one will receive:

Charities	Donation
________________	$ ________
________________	$ ________

Name: Date:

Charity

Design a poster to raise awareness for a charitable organization.

Remember to be more informative by using pictures or words.

Tips for Making a Poster:

- create a catchy, easy-to-remember slogan
- explain what the organization is and how it helps
- focus on what the need is
- focus on how the organization helps those in need

Name: Date:

Charity

Read the quotation. Then answer the question.

> *"A bone to the dog is not charity. Charity is the bone shared with the dog, when you are just as hungry as the dog."*
>
> *– Jack London*

Do you agree with how Jack London defined charity? Why or why not?

Name: Date:

Perseverance

A Persevering Caterpillar (I)

There once was a caterpillar who wanted to be a butterfly. He was roly-poly, dull, and hairy, and he was getting plumper every day. But he felt as though he was meant to fly.

"All I do is munch and crunch. I don't like munching and I don't like crunching!" said the caterpillar. He steadied himself on the leaf as a butterfly fluttered teasingly by.

So the caterpillar persevered. As much as he disliked the taste of parsley, he knew he had to eat it. He hated how round he was getting, but everyone told him it was part of becoming a butterfly.

One day, just as he was starting to feel like he was as big as an elephant and couldn't possibly eat anymore, the caterpillar had the urge to stop. Winds were blowing colder and more often now. The butterflies had all gone, perhaps to wherever the flowers had gone, he thought. All that munching and all that crunching, and all the caterpillar got was fat. Now he had to endure a long, hungry winter.

Name: Date:

Perseverance

A Persevering Caterpillar (II)

Which is what he did. Wrapped up in his cozy home for one, the caterpillar went through a miraculous change that winter. His steadfast feasting really did pay off. When the air was warm and calm, when the flowers came out of their winter hide-away, the caterpillar did not come out to munch and crunch. But he did flutter gracefully by.

Perseverance is sticking with something despite difficulties.

The caterpillar in the story found it difficult to hold on to his dream of becoming a butterfly. It seemed to him he was moving in the opposite direction, becoming a bigger, rounder caterpillar, instead of a graceful, fluttering butterfly. How hard it must have been for him to keep munching and crunching! We know that he would not have ever become a butterfly, though, if he had stopped eating.

Perseverance is a character trait that helps people meet their goals. We must remember that most people do not achieve great things without great difficulty. We should expect to make mistakes when we try new things, and we should learn from them and try again. Perseverance helps us do that.

Name: Date:

Perseverance

Give an example for each situation below.

Perseverance is something we use for little and big things. Teaching your little sister to catch a ball in an afternoon can take perseverance, as can learning a new language, which takes years.

1. A time when you have persevered or are persevering:

2. A time when you gave up on something, and wish you had persevered:

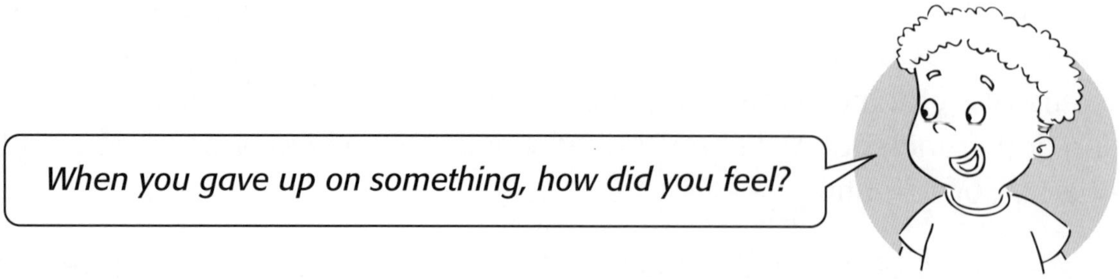

Name: Date:

Perseverance

Write your advice on the lines.

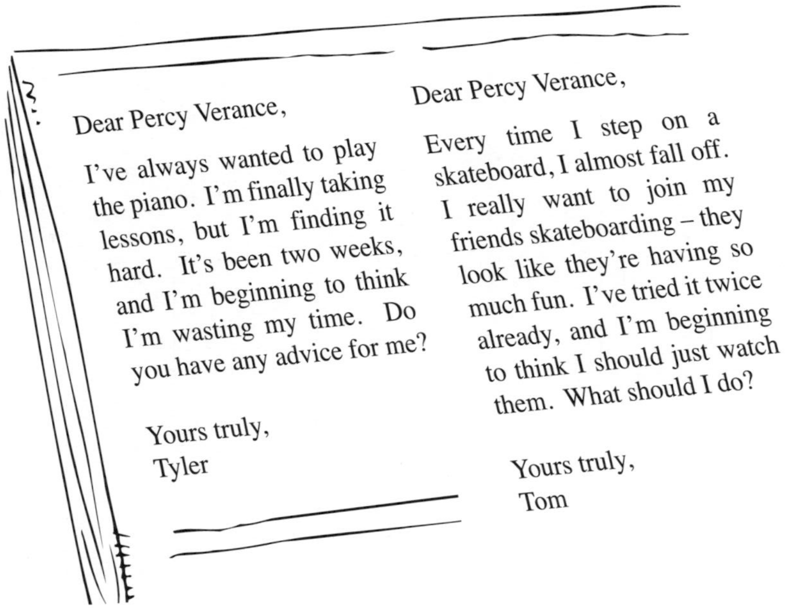
Dear Percy Verance,

I've always wanted to play the piano. I'm finally taking lessons, but I'm finding it hard. It's been two weeks, and I'm beginning to think I'm wasting my time. Do you have any advice for me?

Yours truly,
Tyler

Dear Percy Verance,

Every time I step on a skateboard, I almost fall off. I really want to join my friends skateboarding – they look like they're having so much fun. I've tried it twice already, and I'm beginning to think I should just watch them. What should I do?

Yours truly,
Tom

Dear Tyler,

Yours truly,

Dear Tom,

Yours truly,

Name: Date:

Perseverance

Keep a journal for a week to record your levels of perseverence regarding different activities. Then answer the questions.

Perseverance Awareness Log

Week starting from: ____________

date month year

	Activities	Level of Perseverance (high, moderate, low)
Sun		____________
Mon		____________
Tue		____________
Wed		____________
Thu		____________
Fri		____________
Sat		____________

In what areas can you have more perseverance? How can you achieve that?

____

____

Name: Date:

Perseverance

Write a paragraph about someone's perseverance in reaching a goal. You can write about a family member, someone else you know, or someone you've read about.

Guiding questions:

- Whose story is it?
- What was the person's goal?
- What difficulties did he/she come across?
- How did he/she overcome these difficulties?
- How long did it take him/her to reach the goal?
- What does this story mean to you?

____________________ 's Perseverance

Name: Date:

Tolerance

Tolerance comes from a willingness to accept that others are different from us.

When we see someone whose skin colour is not ours, or whose physical ability is not the same as ours, do we see mainly the differences between us? Or do we also see the similarities between us? Usually, there are many more similarities between people than there are differences. The person with a different skin colour than you may like airplanes just like you do, and he or she may laugh at the same types of jokes or enjoy summer more than winter, just like you.

To be tolerant, we cannot be afraid of differences. Learning about different cultures and meeting different kinds of people goes a long way in developing tolerance. The more we know about people and their differences, the less fear we have of them.

Name: Date:

Tolerance

Write the name of a person who is different from you in each of the following ways. Then find something you have in common.

Joe is in Grade 5, and I'm in Grade 6. We're in different grades, but we both like drawing.

Different race: ____________________ and I

What we have in common: ____________________

____

Different cultural background: ____________________ and I

What we have in common: ____________________

____

Different age: ____________________ and I

What we have in common: ____________________

____

Different gender: ____________________ and I

What we have in common: ____________________

____

Different intellectual strengths: ____________________ and I

What we have in common: ____________________

____

Different physical abilities: ____________________ and I

What we have in common: ____________________

____

Name: Date:

Tolerance

Answer Ginny's question. Then give two examples to support your argument.

Example 1

Example 2

Name: Date:

Tolerance

Write the definitions of the words below. Then give an example of each of these forms of intolerance.

1. Definition of ***Prejudice***: ____________________

   Example: ____________________

   ____

2. Definition of ***Bigotry***: ____________________

   Example: ____________________

   ____

3. Definition of ***Discrimination***: ____________________

   Example: ____________________

   ____

   ____

   ____

   ____

Name: Date:

Tolerance

Think about your own exposure to differences in people and how you react to the differences. Put a checkmark beside the statements that apply to you.

Measuring My Tolerance

- ❍ I know people from different cultures.
- ❍ I learn about different cultural celebrations in my community.
- ❍ I try foods from different cultures when I have the opportunity.
- ❍ I read about cultures that are different from mine.
- ❍ I like to meet new people.
- ❍ I include people who are different from me in my circle of friends.
- ❍ The movies I watch include those made by people from different cultures.
- ❍ I know that other people have opinions that are different from my opinions.
- ❍ When I meet new people, I see and appreciate both the differences and similarities between us.
- ❍ I know that other people have likes and dislikes that are different from my likes and dislikes.

Do you think you're a tolerant person?

Name: Date:

Tolerance

Read the quotation. Then answer the questions.

> *"In the practice of tolerance, one's enemy is the best teacher."*
>
> *– Dalai Lama*

In what way can an enemy be the best teacher of tolerance?

What are three other things that help you develop tolerance?

Name: Date:

Empathy

Elaine was chatting happily with her friends when she noticed a little boy on the ground, holding his knee. Her smile gave way to a look of concern.

"Oh dear," Elaine said, and she knelt down in front of him. "Looks like you've got quite a scrape. That must hurt. Can I help you?"

The little boy felt comforted. His knee still hurt, but there was something soothing in knowing that someone knew how he felt. He nodded his head and allowed himself to lean on Elaine as he got up.

"Thanks," he said. "I'm okay now."

Empathy is understanding and sharing the feelings of others.

The little boy in the story was in pain – in both physical pain from falling and emotional pain from falling in public. Elaine saw his pain, and she probably felt his pain, too. She was able to comfort him with her expression of empathy.

Do you think Elaine felt empathy because she has experienced the same kind of pain? It is easier to be empathetic when we have had a similar experience. However, not having experienced a particular person's type of pain doesn't mean we cannot feel empathy towards him or her. In this case, we must imagine ourselves in the person's shoes.

Name: Date:

Empathy

Look at the pictures. Write a sentence to describe the feeling of the person in each situation.

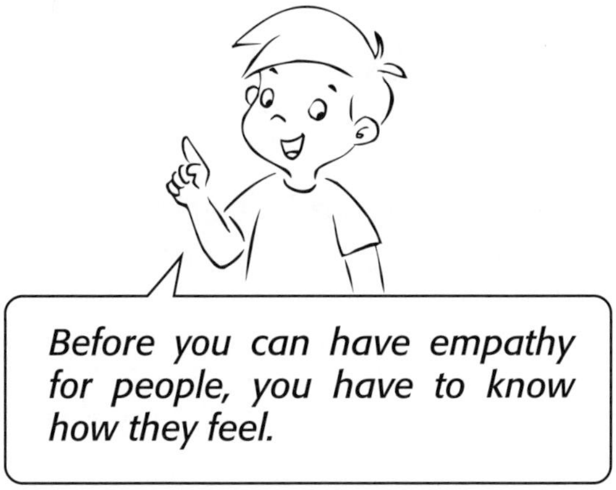

His Feeling

Her Feeling

His Feeling

Her Feeling

Name: Date:

Empathy

Write about an experience in which your friend showed empathy towards you. Then answer the questions.

My Friend's Empathy towards Me

1. In the above experience, how did you feel?

2. Did it help when your friend showed empathy towards you?

3. What advantages do you think your friend had in showing empathy towards you?

4. Did respect and tolerance have anything to do with this experience?

Name: Date:

Empathy

Some philosophers believe that reading novels can help one develop empathy towards others in the real world.

Do you agree with this? Why or why not?

Do you think watching movies can build a person's empathy in a similar way?

Name: Date:

Empathy

Write about an incident in which you put yourself in another's shoes, that is, showed your empathy towards someone.

Kim, I understand how you're feeling.

I put myself in ____________________ 's shoes.

____

____

____

____

____

____

____

____

____

____

____

____

____

Name: Date:

Empathy

Read the quotation. Draw pictures of the people and write their names in the boxes. Answer the questions.

> *"The words 'It must have been' are magical words that say to the other, 'I understand how it was.' "*
>
> ***– Gerry Spence***

Think of two people who showed empathy towards you. What did they say?

Now think of two people to whom you showed empathy. What did you say?

Name: Date:

Self-discipline

Self-discipline is being in control of our own actions.

Self-discipline can be most difficult when we have strong feelings about something. Anger, for example, can cause us to behave in ways that hurt other people. Self-discipline means that even though we can feel angry, we should behave in a productive way and not in a destructive way.

Strong feelings, without self-discipline, can make us forget our responsibilities or our sense of right and wrong. If we have self-discipline, we can have strong feelings and still be in control of ourselves.

Name: Date:

Self-discipline

Write the rules for the places below. Add one more place where there is a set of rules to follow.

Family Rules

- ______________________________
- ______________________________
- ______________________________

School Rules

- ______________________________
- ______________________________
- ______________________________
- ______________________________

__________ Rules

- ______________________________
- ______________________________
- ______________________________
- ______________________________

Name: Date:

Self-discipline

Think of two places: one where you find rules easy to follow; the other where rules are more difficult to follow. Draw the two places and write sentences.

A Place with Rules Easy to Follow:

Reasons: ______________________________

____

____

____

Are you self-disciplined there?

____

____

A Place with Rules Difficult to Follow:

Reasons: ______________________________

____

____

____

Are you self-disciplined there?

____

____

Name: Date:

Self-discipline

Compare your actions with and without self-discipline in each situation.

Listening to a long speech at an assembly

With Self-discipline

Without Self-discipline

Knowing a secret that others don't know

With Self-discipline

Without Self-discipline

Name: Date:

Self-discipline

Think of a bad habit you would like to stop. Keep a week's record of whether or not you were self-disciplined enough to stop doing it each day.

Self-discipline helps us stop bad habits such as nail-biting and watching too much TV.

A bad habit that I would like to stop:

____

My One-week Record

Sunday (____________): with / without self-discipline

Monday (____________): with / without self-discipline

Tuesday (____________): with / without self-discipline

Wednesday (____________): with / without self-discipline

Thursday (____________): with / without self-discipline

Friday (____________): with / without self-discipline

Saturday (____________): with / without self-discipline

Was I self-disciplined enough to stop this bad habit?

____

Name: Date:

Self-discipline

Read the quotation. Then answer the question.

> *"Self-discipline begins with the mastery of your thoughts. If you don't control what you think, you can't control what you do. Simply, self-discipline enables you to think first and act afterward."*
>
> *- Napoleon Hill*

Write two incidents in which self-discipline enabled you to think first and act afterward.

Incident 1

Incident 2

Name: Date:

Patience

Patience can be a lot of things, but it is, above all, an endurance test. Can you listen to all sides of an argument? Could you wait for a dilly-dallying friend? Have you managed to stay calm, even when your birthday is a few days away? Do you keep from getting frustrated when you can't figure out your math homework? If you've answered yes to a few, or all, of these questions, then you are a very patient person.

Patience can be a hard trait to develop, and it takes a lot of work to be a patient person. There are things you can do to help stay patient in most situations. Getting your mind off of what you are waiting for is often the best way to stay patient, so read a book, play a game, or talk with your friends or family to help pass the time. It also helps to remind yourself, in the case of being patient with others, that you would want them to be patient with you if the situation was reversed. Being patient shows that you have self-control and that you respect and understand others.

Name: Date:

Patience

Complete the sentence to examine each of the situations about patience.

I have a hard time being patient when I teach my brother.

1. I have a hard time being patient when ______

2. At home, I am patient when ______

3. I am patient at school when ______

4. I was treated with patience when ______

5. I wish I were treated with more patience when ______

6. To be patient, it helps if I ______

Name: Date:

Patience

Plan a day to be your most patient. At the end of that day, check off the things you were able to do.

My Day of
Patience

At home, I will

- ______________________
- ______________________
- ______________________

At school, I will

- ______________________
- ______________________
- ______________________

At __________, I will

- ______________________
- ______________________
- ______________________

Will you be more patient tomorrow?

Name: Date:

Patience

Strategies to Increase Patience:

- **speak calmly**
- **count from one to ten in your head**
- **think before you act**
- **look for a compromise**
- **talk to an adult**

Read the situations below. Write how you would patiently handle each situation.

1. Your older sister takes so much time in the bathroom that you are almost late for school every morning.

2. You've only received $2 in two weeks in your effort to raise funds for the upcoming dance-a-thon. You wonder if it's even worth trying.

Name: Date:

Patience

Write about an unhappy experience caused by your impatience.

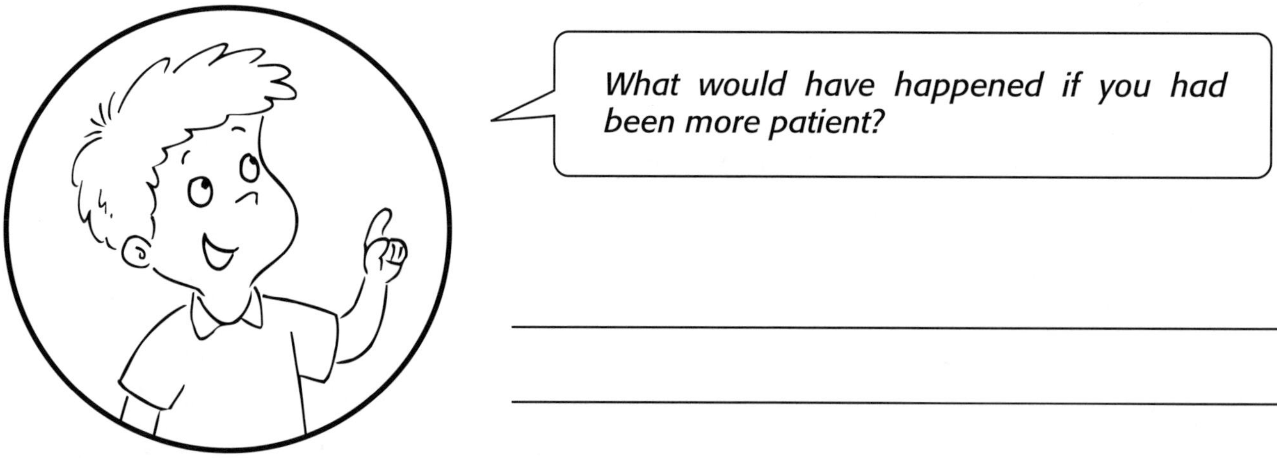

Name: Date:

Patience

Write the meaning of this proverb. Then give two examples that support this idea, one from yourself and one from your parents.

All good things come to he who waits.

Meaning: ______________________________

____

My Example

____

My Parents' Example

____

Name: Date:

Loyalty

When we are loyal to something, we are committed to it. It may be an ideal, like freedom, or an organization, like your school. Even more often, though, we are loyal to people.

Our families have our loyalty even if we don't always get along or don't always agree with everything they do. Our friends, especially the person we call our "best" friend, are people we are loyal to. If we weren't, they wouldn't be our friends. Loyalty means we are there when they need us. We don't abandon them because we've made new friends, and we keep their confidence when necessary. Of course, we should always use our judgment about keeping some things secret. A loyal friend shouldn't keep a friend's secret if he or she believes telling an adult would help.

Loyalty is also about following the rules and laws of the places you are loyal to. This kind of loyalty helps keep a place enjoyable for everyone.

More than anything else, we should always be loyal to ourselves. This means knowing what we want and going after it, and believing that we are capable of getting it, as well as worthy of having it. If we are not loyal to ourselves, how can anyone else be loyal to us?

Name: Date:

Loyalty

Write how you show loyalty to your family and your friends.

Loyalty to My Family

- ______________________
- ______________________
- ______________________
- ______________________
- ______________________
- ______________________

Loyalty to My Friends

- ______________________
- ______________________
- ______________________
- ______________________
- ______________________
- ______________________

Name: Date:

Loyalty

Think of a place you think you are loyal to. Write a list of rules that you have to follow there. Then put a checkmark in the circle to show how often you follow each rule.

Place I'm Loyal to ______________________

Rules

How Often I Follow These Rules

Rules	Always	Usually	Often	Sometimes	Seldom
• ______	○	○	○	○	○
• ______	○	○	○	○	○
• ______	○	○	○	○	○
• ______	○	○	○	○	○
• ______	○	○	○	○	○
• ______	○	○	○	○	○

How did you score? Did you answer "always" for each rule? If not, why?

____

____

Name: Date:

Loyalty

Write about an incident in which you spoke ill of a friend. Why did you do so? How did you feel afterwards?

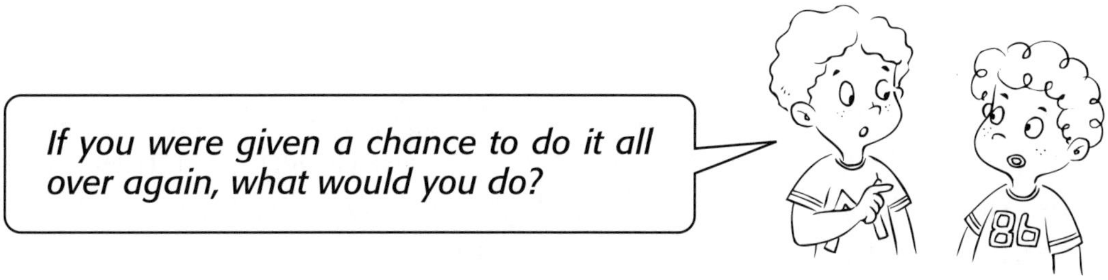

Name: Date:

Loyalty

Look at each of the scenarios below. Write what action the child should take to be loyal to himself or herself.

1. Jess loves gymnastics, and has been practising it since she was five. She has to make a decision: her coach wants her to increase her hours of training, but she has recently joined a marimba band. She doesn't enjoy it as much as gymnastics, but she knows the band really needs her. What should Jess do?

2. Ben has a chance to become friends with a group of popular boys in his school. As long as they don't find out where he lives – a run-down apartment building, he's pretty sure they will accept him. One day, the boys want to meet at Ben's place before going to the pool. What should Ben do?

Name: Date:

Loyalty

Read the quotation. Then complete the exercise.

> *"The greater the loyalty of a group toward the group, the greater is the motivation among the members to achieve the goals of the group, and the greater the probability that the group will achieve its goals."*
>
> ***– Walter Winchell***

1. Think of a group you have joined (for example, a basketball team). Write about things you can do to show loyalty to the group.

2. Write about an incident in which the loyalty of all members of your group helped achieve a goal.

Forgiveness

A Cat and Two Mice (I)

A cat that failed to catch two mice,
Said some words that were not nice,
"When next you leave your mousy hole,
I'll put you in my cat food bowl!"

The little mice had heard enough,
What kitty said was hurtful stuff!
All day they planned their tit for tat,
By gum! They'd teach that naughty cat!

The mice stirred up a mousy stew,
When their feelings calmed, they stirred anew,
They thought of names they'd call the cat –
Hairy Fur Ball! Stinky Rat!

Name: Date:

Forgiveness

A Cat and Two Mice (II)

But then, the mice, they thought it through,
Their wicked thoughts did not undo
The feline's mean and nasty curse,
In fact, it made them feel much worse.

Sure, what the kitty did was bad,
But why were they still mad?
What good could come from retribution?
What comfort? What solution?

If those two mice would hold a grudge,
If spiteful feelings could not budge,
The kitty's words would hurt the mice,
Not just once, but twice.

In this story, the mice were upset by the cat's threat. They spent a lot of time thinking their own nasty thoughts about the cat after that. Did it make them feel better? Maybe it did at first. But eventually they found that their thoughts of revenge made them unhappy.

When the mice let their ill will towards the cat take over their thoughts, they were living with anger and discontent. It is normal to have those feelings when we are hurt, but we hurt ourselves even more by holding onto them.

Forgiveness is as good for the forgiver as it is for the one being forgiven.

Name: Date:

Forgiveness

Write a journal entry about something that happened to you that needed or still needs your forgiveness.

Forgiving does not mean we should deny that what was done hurt us and our feelings. In fact, acknowledging the misdeed and our feelings about it is a step to forgiveness. Keeping a journal helps us do this.

My Journal

Date: ____________________

Name: Date:

Forgiveness

Write a journal entry about something that happened to you in which you needed someone's forgiveness.

My Journal

Date:

Name: Date:

Forgiveness

Answer the questions.

How does it feel to forgive?

____

How does being a forgiving person benefit you?

____

How does it feel to be forgiven?

____

Name: Date:

Forgiveness

Read the quotation. Then answer the questions.

> ***"It is easier to forgive an enemy than to forgive a friend."***
>
> ***– William Blake***

1. Do you think that forgiving an enemy is easier than forgiving a friend? Why or why not?

____

____

____

____

____

____

2. Write about an experience in which you forgave an enemy, and one in which you forgave a friend.

____

____

____

____

____

____

Name: Date:

Reliability

Reliability is:

- doing what we promise to do
- not making any promises if we think we will not be able to fulfil them
- completing tasks on time
- doing our very best to carry out our responsibilities
- always being there for a friend in need
- listening to our friends even if we're not able to help
- being where we're supposed to be at the right time

When we don't make the effort to arrive on time, we inconvenience others as well as ourselves.

People depend on us to be reliable in our attendance, our work habits, and the quality of our work. Being reliable means we are trustworthy, honest, and responsible, so people can always count on us.

If we want to be successful in every aspect of our lives, we should always try to keep our word.

Name: Date:

Reliability

Keep a journal for a few days, writing down the people you relied on and what you relied on them for.

- *Think of the people you count on or those who come through for you when you need it most.*
- *It could be a sibling, a teacher, a friend, or your parents.*

Person I Relied on: What I Relied Him or Her for

__________ : __________

__________ : __________

__________ : __________

__________ : __________

__________ : __________

__________ : __________

__________ : __________

Name: Date:

Reliability

Complete the chart below about how you show reliability in different areas of your life.

I am Reliable...

at home

at school

How can you be more reliable?

Name: Date:

Reliability

Being organized helps us to be reliable. Include these on your calendar.

- tests you need to study for
- goals to work towards
- due dates of assignments
- appointments
- other things to do

Keep organized with a monthly calendar. Write the days in the squares.

_______________ month _______________ year

Sunday	Monday	Tuesday	Wednesday	Thursday	Friday	Saturday

Name: Date:

Reliability

Write a letter of recognition to a person you rely on. Explain what his or her reliability means to you.

Recognition of Reliability

Dear ______________________ ,

From,

____

Name: Date:

Reliability

Read the quotation. Then answer the questions.

> ***"The shift of fortune tests the reliability of friends."***
>
> ***– Marcus Tullius Cicero***

1. Do you agree with the above quotation? Why or why not?

2. Do you have a reliable friend? In what way is he or she reliable?

Does he or she think that you are a reliable friend, too?

Name: Date:

Gratitude

Gratitude is more than expressing thanks to someone who has done something nice for you. It is a way of thinking that allows us to live each day in appreciation, no matter what our troubles are. It is looking on the bright side.

Gratitude is perhaps the most important of all virtues, as it enables us to develop all the others. Honesty, punctuality, generosity, and other good character traits are easier to come by if we have gratitude.

Living our life with gratitude shows great respect for those around us, our environment, and ourselves.

Name: Date:

Gratitude

Make a list of everything you are grateful for and the person you wish to show gratitude to. Try to fill every line.

something I'm grateful for

someone I wish to show gratitude to

Name: Date:

Gratitude

Write how you show gratitude. Try to write a different way for each situation.

1. A stranger lets you know that you've dropped a book.

   Way to Show Gratitude: ____________________

2. A cyclist stops and waits to let you cross the street.

   Way to Show Gratitude: ____________________

3. You receive a gift from an out-of-town relative.

   Way to Show Gratitude: ____________________

4. You receive extra help with homework from a teacher.

   Way to Show Gratitude: ____________________

5. A classmate gives you some jelly beans from her bag of jelly beans.

   Way to Show Gratitude:

   ____

   ____

6. You receive a compliment from a friend.

   Way to Show Gratitude:

   ____

   ____

Name: Date:

Gratitude

Write about an incident in which you found it hard to express your gratitude.

Why was it hard to express your gratitude?

Name: Date:

Gratitude

Find a public expression of gratitude from a newspaper. Cut it out and paste it below.

Expressions of gratitude are made public when they are published in special sections of local newspapers. They can be long paragraphs listing details and all the people they are thanking, or just sentence-long expressions of appreciation for a small, anonymous gesture.

Notice of
Thanks

Think of someone you would like to thank publicly. Write your own notice of thanks.

Name: Date:

Gratitude

Read what the children say. Then complete the exercise.

1. Make a list of things that you have taken for granted.

- ______________________________
- ______________________________
- ______________________________
- ______________________________
- ______________________________

2. Give an example that illustrates Cynthia Ozick's quotation about gratitude.

____

____

____

____

____

Name: Date:

Friendship

To have friends, we must be a friend. We must be trustworthy and kind, helpful and honest, as well as cooperative with and loyal to our friends. Friends listen and share, and can be relied on to do what is best.

Friends like to be with each other, but they give each other time to be with others as well. Friendships need space for growing and time for blossoming. Good friendships are not found, but built.

Founded on the deepest trust

Reliable at all times

Immeasurable love and patience

Endless respect and forgiveness

Never-ending care and support

Distance not a problem at all

Slow to criticize in front of others

Hearty praises come in time

Indispensable like air and water

Precious gift of life for sure

Name: Date:

Friendship

Answer the following questions.

1. What is the difference between an acquaintance and a friend?

2. Is "having a friend" the same as "being a friend"? Why or why not?

3. Do you know what "fair-weather friend" means?

Do you want any fair-weather friends? Why or why not?

Name: Date:

Friendship

Paste a photo or draw a picture of you with your friends below. Then complete the sentences.

My Friends & Me

1. Things we have in common include ______

2. I like my friends because ______

3. My friends like me because ______

Name: Date:

Friendship

Write what you think an ideal friend should do.

Things that an Ideal Friend Should Do:

Can you do all of the above? Are you an ideal friend?

If you want to have an ideal friend, you'll need to be an ideal friend first.

Name: Date:

Friendship

Check the character traits you have. Then answer the questions.

Friend

- ❍ kind
- ❍ loving
- ❍ patient
- ❍ generous
- ❍ helpful
- ❍ trustworthy
- ❍ cooperative
- ❍ respectful
- ❍ honest
- ❍ loyal
- ❍ sincere

Foe

- ❍ unkind
- ❍ jealous
- ❍ impatient
- ❍ greedy
- ❍ unhelpful
- ❍ deceitful
- ❍ uncooperative
- ❍ disrespectful
- ❍ dishonest
- ❍ disloyal
- ❍ insincere

Are you a great friend? What can you do to build stronger friendships?

___

___

___

Name: Date:

Friendship

Read the quotation. Then answer the questions.

> *"A real friend is one who walks in when the rest of the world walks out."*
>
> *– Walter Winchell*

1. Rewrite the quotation above in your own words.

2. Write about an incident in which your friend walked in when the rest of the world walked out.

Name: Date:

Responsibility

Being responsible means doing the right thing in a particular situation.

We can be responsible about the way we treat other people, as well as about our interactions with others. Speaking with respect, being patient, and being punctual is being responsible.

Doing work of which we are capable, and doing it well, is also a form of responsibility. When we carry out our responsibilities at home, and everyone else does, too, things run smoothly, giving all family members more time for leisure and fun.

Our responsibilities change as our lives change. As we grow and learn new things, we can take on new responsibilities. When we are given a new opportunity – a new responsibility – we should take it seriously. When we do, our responsibility gives back to us. We become known as responsible people, and are given even more opportunities.

Name: Date:

Responsibility

Our Unique Responsibilities (I)

A. Many people have unique responsibilities in their community. Read each description and decide who best fits the responsibility.

construction worker | landscaper | teacher | doctor | coach
waste collector | student | park ranger | judge | police officer

1. A ______________________ is responsible for students' education in the classroom.

2. A ______________________ is responsible for his or her team.

3. A ______________________ is responsible for taking care of the sick.

4. A ______________________ is responsible for wild animals and provincial and national parks.

5. 

A ______________________ is responsible for keeping green space look beautiful.

6. 

A ______________________ is responsible for the community's safety.

Name: Date:

Responsibility

Our Unique Responsibilities (II)

7. A ____________________ is responsible for building houses, stores, and roads.

8. A ____________________ is responsible for collecting garbage and recycling.

9. A ____________________ is responsible for upholding the law.

10. A ____________________ is responsible for his or her homework.

B. Answer the questions.

1.

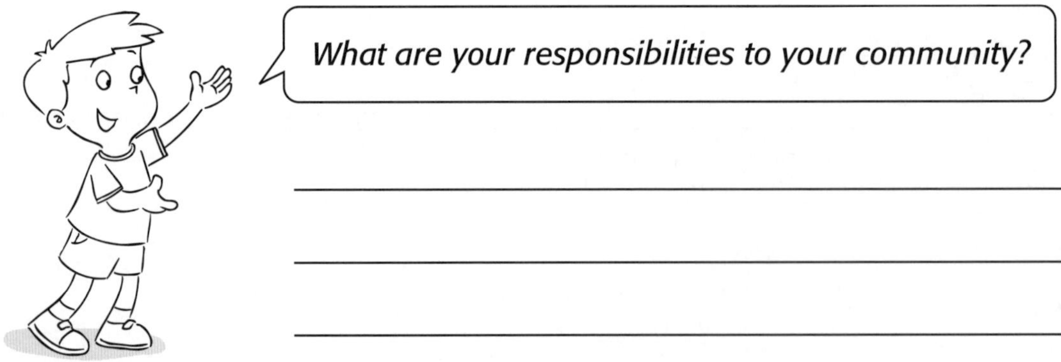

____

____

____

2. How does it feel to have these responsibilities?

____

____

____

Name: Date:

Responsibility

What are your responsibilities in different areas of your life? How does it feel to have these responsibilities? Did you always feel the same about them?

We gain new responsibilities as we mature. As ten- or eleven-year-olds, we are much more capable of being responsible than we were as six- or seven-year-olds.

	Responsibility	Feelings When New	Feelings Now
 **At** home			
 **At** school			

Name: Date:

Responsibility

Read the quotation. Then complete the exercise.

> ***"It is not only for what we do that we are held responsible, but also for what we do not do."***
>
> ***– Moliere***

1. Explain the quotation in your own words.

2. Write about an incident from your own life that explains what the quotation means to you.

Name: Date:

Responsibility

Are you responsible? Keep track of how you are becoming a responsible person. Check the statements that apply to you. Then colour the box that corresponds with the number of checks you have.

Responsibility Checklist

- ○ I record important dates and appointments on a calendar.
- ○ I take responsibility for my mistakes, and I learn from them.
- ○ I listen in class, and ask questions when I'm unsure.
- ○ I don't make excuses for things I have done wrong.
- ○ I arrive on time to places I am supposed to be.
- ○ I list my homework and when it is due in my agenda.
- ○ I do the chores I am responsible for.
- ○ I treat other people with respect.
- ○ I take care of my belongings.
- ○ I return the items I borrow.
- ○ I treat animals with respect.
- ○ I reduce, reuse, and recycle.

How Responsible Are You?

Number of ✓

☐ 10 – 12
a very responsible person

☐ 7 – 9
a responsible person

☐ fewer than 6
You have to work harder to become a more responsible person.

Name: Date:

Courage

Courage is strength.

Courage of the mind, or mental courage, helps us do things that would be easier not to do even though it would be better for us to do them, like studying more than we normally would for an important math test.

Moral courage is doing what is right despite obstacles or pressure to do otherwise. When we refuse to follow the lead of friends who are bullying a second grader, and make an attempt to stop them, we are showing moral courage, or strength of character.

Physical courage is performing a physical act in spite of obstacles such as exhaustion or pain. Jumping over a fence to save your brother from falling into a marsh takes physical courage. Finishing a relay race with your best time, despite having the worst side stitch you've ever had, is neither life-saving nor life-threatening, but takes courage nonetheless.

With physical courage, motivation counts. It is not courageous to put yourself in danger just for fun. That is only foolishness.

Name: Date:

Courage

Read the scenarios. Decide whether the courage is moral, mental, or physical.

1. Caroline, normally shy, speaks in front of the whole class. ____________________

2. Geraldine finally asks her boss for a raise. ____________________

3. Surrinder tells his parents that he was the one who ate a slice of his aunt's birthday cake. ____________________

4. Gus has to get help for his dog quickly; he runs the four kilometres home without stopping. ____________________

5. Tiffany refuses to follow her friends through the orchard; the shortcut will get them to school on time, but she knows that trespassing is wrong. ____________________

6. Gregory swims the last lap of the race for his team; his exhaustion is barely noticeable. ____________________

Name: Date:

Courage

Answer the questions.

1.

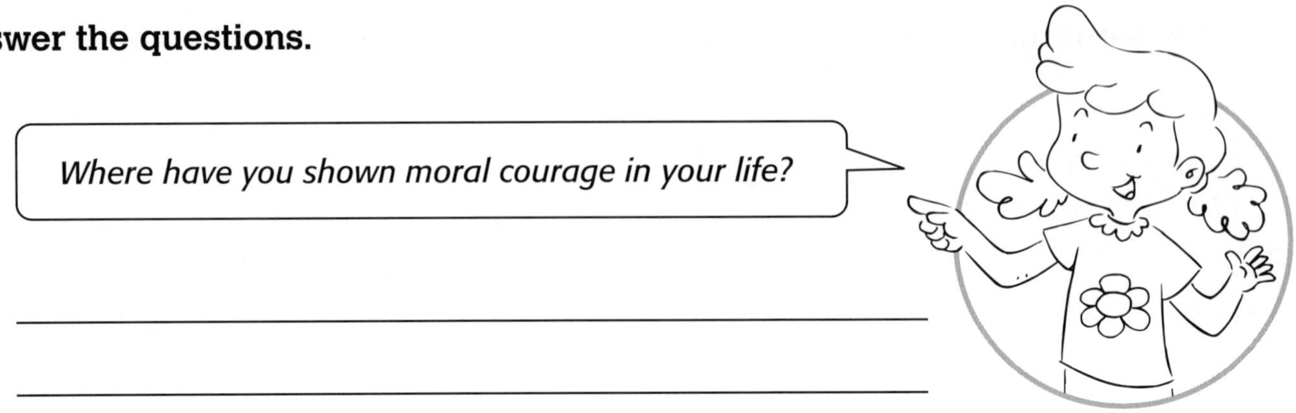

2. Where have you shown mental courage in your life?

3. Where have you shown physical courage in your life?

Name: Date:

Courage

Read the three quotations below. Circle the one that you agree with most and explain what it means in your own words with an example from your own life.

"The best way out is always through."

– Robert Frost

"Courage is the ladder on which all other virtues mount."

– Clare Booth Luce

"Courage is the discovery that you may not win, and trying when you know you can lose."

– Tom Krause

I've circled the quotation that I agree with most. To me, it means:

____

____

____

____

____

My Example

____

____

____

____

Name: Date:

Courage

For many, certain animals are symbols of courage. Think of an animal that you think symbolizes courage, and answer the questions.

1. Which animal symbolizes courage for you?

____

2. Why does it symbolize courage?

____

____

____

3. Imagine yourself as that animal. Will doing so help you find courage in difficult situations? Why or why not?

____

____

____

____

Name: Date:

Courage

Think of an act of courage you've witnessed. It does not have to be an act that would make the news. Write a newspaper article about it. Create a short, catchy headline, and draw a picture that illustrates the act. Don't forget that all good news is objective (reports only the facts), and answers the questions, "who", "what", "where", "when", and "why".

The Daily Good News

Name: Date:

Leadership

Leadership is...

listening and communicating well

being trustworthy

service to others

making difficult decisions

having a positive attitude

inspiring others

being willing to follow

We all show leadership in one way or another. We may be leaders in clubs we belong to, or in caring for our pets or our younger siblings.

Likewise, we all have a leader in some way. All the qualities listed above are found in good leaders, including the last one: being willing to follow. Even leaders need leadership sometimes, and do well to follow those they can learn from.

Name: Date:

Leadership

It takes many character traits to be a leader. Find and circle the characteristics of a leader. Think of a person who shows leadership qualities. Then decide which character traits that person has.

The person who shows leadership might be you.

The Characteristics of a Leader

trustworthiness unkind respect responsibility dishonesty loyal

irresponsible self-disciplined responsible dishonest reliable

helpful disrespectful flexible self-indulgent confident creative

persevering ambitious resourceful stubborn courageous

diligent selfish

A person who shows leadership is...

Name: Date:

Leadership

Which picture in each pair depicts leadership? Check the correct circle. Then write a sentence explaining how that person is showing leadership.

1.

A

B

2.

A

B

Name: Date:

Leadership

Answer the questions.

1. *Do you think everyone shows leadership in some way? Explain.*

2. Can someone be a leader all the time? Why or why not?

3. How does being willing to follow show good leadership?

4. In what way do you show leadership?

Name: Date:

Leadership

Design a certificate to award to someone who shows good leadership skills. Choose one of the quotations to write on the certificate. Then complete the certificate and give it to the deserving person.

"If your actions inspire others to dream more, learn more, do more and become more, you are a leader."

– John Quincy Adams

"You cannot be a leader, and ask other people to follow you, unless you know how to follow, too."

– Sam Rayburn

Leadership Award

Date: ______________________

To: ______________________

From: ______________________

You show leadership by ______________________________________

____

Quotation " ______________________________________

______________________________________ "

– ______________________

Name: Date:

Leadership

Read the scenario. Then answer the questions.

Four of you are asked to do a group assignment. All of you are responsible for completing one task that will contribute to the whole, but one of you must lead the project to ensure that everything gets done and the project is a unified whole.

1. How would you feel if you were chosen to be the leader? How would you lead the group?

____

____

____

____

2. How would you feel if you were not chosen to be the leader? How would you show your support for the leader and for the other members of the group?

____

____

____

____

Name: Date:

Ambition

These headlines from the past are examples of historic ambitions – examples of what people can achieve when they are ambitious!

Ambition is a character trait that can lead to great things. If it were not for ambitious people, we would be without much of the technological and medical advancements we enjoy today.

Ambition is a strong desire, determination, and a dream all mixed in one.

Name: Date:

Ambition

Finish the sentences to help determine what your ambitions are.

1. I am interested in ______________________________

2. I am curious about ______________________________

3. Issues I'm concerned about are ______________________________

4. From what you've written, decide on an area where you are most ambitious and come up with a plan that will help you achieve a short-term goal (a few weeks to a year) in that area.

My Plan for Achieving My Goal

Name: Date:

Ambition

Answer the questions.

1. Is ambition always a good thing? Why or why not?

2. Are there times when other characteristics, such as honesty and loyalty, should come before ambition?

> *I want to be the captain of my basketball team, and so does my friend. She is a better player than I am, and knows more about basketball. Loyalty to my friend and honesty with myself should come before ambition.*

3. My example of when ______ (characteristic) comes before ambition:

Name: Date:

Ambition

Read what Ivan says. Then record the ambitions of your friends and family members. Write who inspires you the most.

Ambitions can be small or large or anywhere in between. They may be achieved in an hour or in a lifetime. The important thing is that we have them. Sometimes other people's ambitions can inspire our own.

	Name	Ambition
Friends		
Family Members		

_______________ inspires me most because _______________

____

____

Name: Date:

Ambition

There are many characteristics that fuel our ambitions. Check the ones listed below that you believe you have, and add two more of your own.

Ambition Checklist

____ I try my best.

____ I am resourceful.

____ I have self-discipline.

____ I have perseverance.

____ I have self-confidence.

____ I write down my goals.

____ I learn from my mistakes.

____ I get things done on time.

____ I want to do something great.

____ I know that failure often comes before success.

____ I know what my strengths and weaknesses are.

✔ ________________________________

✔ ________________________________

"Far away there in the sunshine are my highest aspirations. I may not reach them, but I can look up and see their beauty, believe in them, and try to follow them."

– Louisa May Alcott

Name: Date:

Ambition

Think about your biggest, long-term ambitions. Write them down on this sheet. Cut it out, fold it up, and put it in an envelope. Tuck it away somewhere safe. (Perhaps you could even ask your parents to hold onto it for you.) Go back to it sometime in the future and see how close you've come. It may help if you write an action plan detailing the steps you need to take to achieve your ambitions, but keep that sheet with you.

Name: Date:

Resourcefulness

An Old Pirate's Treasure (I)

Kevin and Courtney have heard there is an old pirate's treasure buried in the backyard of their new house. Their backyard is almost as big as a football field – how will they ever find it?

"First, we need a map!" said Kevin. "Let's go see Mr. Hookhand. He's an expert on buried pirate treasure."

Indeed, Mr. Hookhand had just the map they were looking for.

Back in the yard, Kevin and Courtney studied the treasure map. Courtney said, "According to the map, this is where the treasure is buried. Let's dig!"

The children looked at each other. "Dig with what?" they said at the same time.

Courtney ran into the house and came back with an old dustpan. "This was meant for sweeping dust, but it will do as a digger today."

Kevin and Courtney dug, but soon they were tired and realized they would have to get help if they were going to find the treasure before supper.

Name: Date:

Resourcefulness

An Old Pirate's Treasure (II)

"There are Tori and Cody! Let's ask them to help us!"

Tori and Cody were happy to help. The four children scooped and shovelled until they hit something hard.

In the story, Kevin and Courtney were resourceful first when they found an expert to help them find a map for the pirate treasure. Then, when they realized they didn't have shovels for digging, they were resourceful enough to find similar tools that could do the job, if not quite as well. Finally, Kevin and Courtney were resourceful in asking for help with the digging.

Resourcefulness is finding a way to do something, even if you don't have the normal tools you would need to get it done. When we solve a problem, or find out what we need to know in order to solve that problem, we are being resourceful.

Name: Date:

Resourcefulness

Finish the story. Describe Kevin and Courtney's resourcefulness in their method of solving the problem of getting the treasure out of the ground.

An Old Pirate's Treasure (III)

Name: Date:

Resourcefulness

Put a checkmark beside the statements that are true for you. Then write an example of you doing each one, and answer the question.

It is true for me (✔).

1. 

I use the dictionary as a resource to find the spelling or meaning of a word. ◯

e.g. ______________________

2. I use encyclopedias and other books as resources for information. ◯

e.g. ______________________

3. I have people in my life that I can use as resources. ◯

e.g. ______________________

4. I am not afraid to ask questions about things I don't know. ◯

e.g. ______________________

5. If I can't immediately solve a problem, I'll try to think of another way. ◯

e.g. ______________________

6. 

Do you think that you are resourceful?

____

Name: Date:

Resourcefulness

Write down two of your goals. Then write some resources you can use to help you reach your goals, and answer the questions.

My Goal: ____________________

Resources: ____________________

____

My Goal: ____________________

Resources: ____________________

____

How is resourcefulness related to creativity?

____

____

____

____

How is resourcefulness related to optimism?

____

____

____

____

Name: Date:

Resourcefulness

Think of a situation where your resourcefulness has benefited the environment, and write it down so that others know they can do it, too. Share ways you are resourceful with your friends, and ask them to share their ways with you.

Being resourceful means finding uses for items that may otherwise be thrown away. It means being environmentally responsible: reusing items, using containers and cloth bags instead of plastic, and not taking more than we need.

An Act of Resourcefulness that Benefited the Environment

Name: Date:

Good Citizenship

There are different ways to show good citizenship. Anything we do that strengthens or helps the community we live in shows good citizenship.

We all belong to many communities. Volunteering to clean your schoolyard helps the smaller community of your school and surrounding neighbourhood. Learning about important issues across the country – a new law, or an upcoming federal election – benefits the very large community of Canada.

Good citizenship means being community-minded: obeying laws and rules, protecting the environment, and being helpful and neighbourly to other citizens.

Name: Date:

Good Citizenship

List the things you do that show good citizenship. Then answer the questions.

Things I Do to Show Good Citizenship

- ____________________
- ____________________
- ____________________
- ____________________
- ____________________

How does your good citizenship benefit others?

____

____

____

____

How does others' good citizenship benefit you?

____

____

____

____

Name: Date:

Good Citizenship

Sort the acts of good citizenship into the correct categories. Write the letters on the lines.

A

B

C

D

E

F

Activism	Obedience to Laws and Rules	National Pride
________	________	________

Name: Date:

Good Citizenship

Think about what you can do to be a good citizen. Brainstorm with your friends some of the needs of your community (country, town, neighbourhood) and school.

The Needs of My Community or School

What can I do to help out?

Name: Date:

Good Citizenship

How well do you know your national anthem? Write in the missing words of "O Canada".

O Canada

O ______ ! Our ______ and native ______ !

______ patriot ______ in all thy sons ______ .

With ______ hearts we see thee ______ ,

The ______ North strong and ______ !

From ______ and ______ O ______ ,

We ______ on ______ for ______ .

God ______ our ______ glorious and ______ !

O Canada, we ______ on ______ for thee.

______ , ______________________ .

Name: Date:

Good Citizenship

Award a Good Citizenship Certificate to a deserving classmate. Explain why he or she is deserving, and choose one of the quotations below to write on it.

"One generation plants the trees; another gets the shade."

- Chinese proverb

"Three keys to more abundant living: caring about others, daring for others, sharing with others."

- William Arthur Ward

Good Citizenship Award

Date: ____________________

Awarded to: ____________________

From: ____________________

For: ____________________

Quotation:

____

– __________

Name: Date:

Flexibility

Flexibility is the ability to adapt to unexpected situations.

Everyone is flexible, but we all have different degrees of flexibility. Some of us try something new at lunch every day; some of us have the same thing all the time because we know we like it. Some of us have lived in the same home and gone to the same school all our lives, so it may be more difficult for us to make new friends than it would be for someone who has moved often and is always the "new kid". However flexible you may (or may not) think you are, you should always try to be open to new things. Stubbornness is the unreasonable need to stick to the same idea or plan; it is flexibility's opposite. Being able to change our routine and our expectations can be a real advantage to us!

Are you ***Frenda*** *or* ***Brenda*** *?*

Name: Date:

Flexibility

How is flexibility related to the following character traits? What benefits are there if you have both and can combine them?

1. **Creativity & Flexibility** ____________________

   ____

   Benefits: ____________________

   ____

2. **Cooperativeness & Flexibility** ____________________

   ____

   Benefits: ____________________

   ____

3. **Self-confidence & Flexibility** ____________________

   ____

   Benefits: ____________________

   ____

4. **Resourcefulness & Flexibility** ____________________

   ____

   Benefits: ____________________

   ____

Name: Date:

Flexibility

Describe what you would do in each situation. Then answer the question.

1. You want to play one game, but your friend wants to play something else.

2. Your drama teacher wants you to play a character you don't really like in a play.

3. The book you want to read next has been borrowed by another student.

Do you think your answers above show that you are a flexible person? If not, what should you do to increase your flexibility?

Name: Date:

Flexibility

Read what Julie says. Then answer the questions.

We both wanted hamburgers, but the restaurant only had one. We decided to order one hamburger and one sandwich and share both. We were happy because we both had our favourite, and we both got to try something new, too!

1. Can you think of a recent situation where you showed flexibility in thinking or routine? Describe it.

____

____

____

____

____

____

2. How did you, or someone else, benefit from this flexibility?

____

____

____

____

____

____

Name: Date:

Flexibility

Many cultures around the world greatly value flexibility. Read the proverbs, and come up with one of your own. Explain how it relates to your life.

A proverb is a short, memorable saying that expresses a truth or gives a warning.

"Take the world as it is, not as it ought to be."

– German proverb

"If you live in the river, you should make friends with the crocodile."

– Indian proverb

My Proverb: ______________________________

____

– ____________ proverb

How it relates to my life:

____

____

____

Name: Date:

Flexibility

Think of an experience you have had where someone (you or another person) has been unable to show flexibility. Write down the experience. Then rewrite it, changing the story so that the person is flexible.

An Experience **without** **Flexibility**

____

____

____

____

____

____

____

An Experience **Changed** Because of **Flexibility**

____

____

____

____

____

____

____

Name: Date:

Self-confidence

Self-confidence is knowing and liking yourself.

It is not the ability to do everything well. When we are self-confident, we know what we are capable of and what we are not. We are not necessarily more capable than anyone else.

We show our self-confidence in the way we stand up for ourselves. If we are unsure, we allow someone more knowledgeable to help us, or we learn about what we don't know.

People with self-confidence are not afraid of responsibility, and are the people most likely to seek out new responsibilities. When we have self-confidence, we are not afraid to ask for what we deserve.

Name: Date:

Self-confidence

Sometimes another person's self-confidence inspires our own. Find or draw a picture of a person who has a lot of self-confidence. Then write about him or her and follow the instructions.

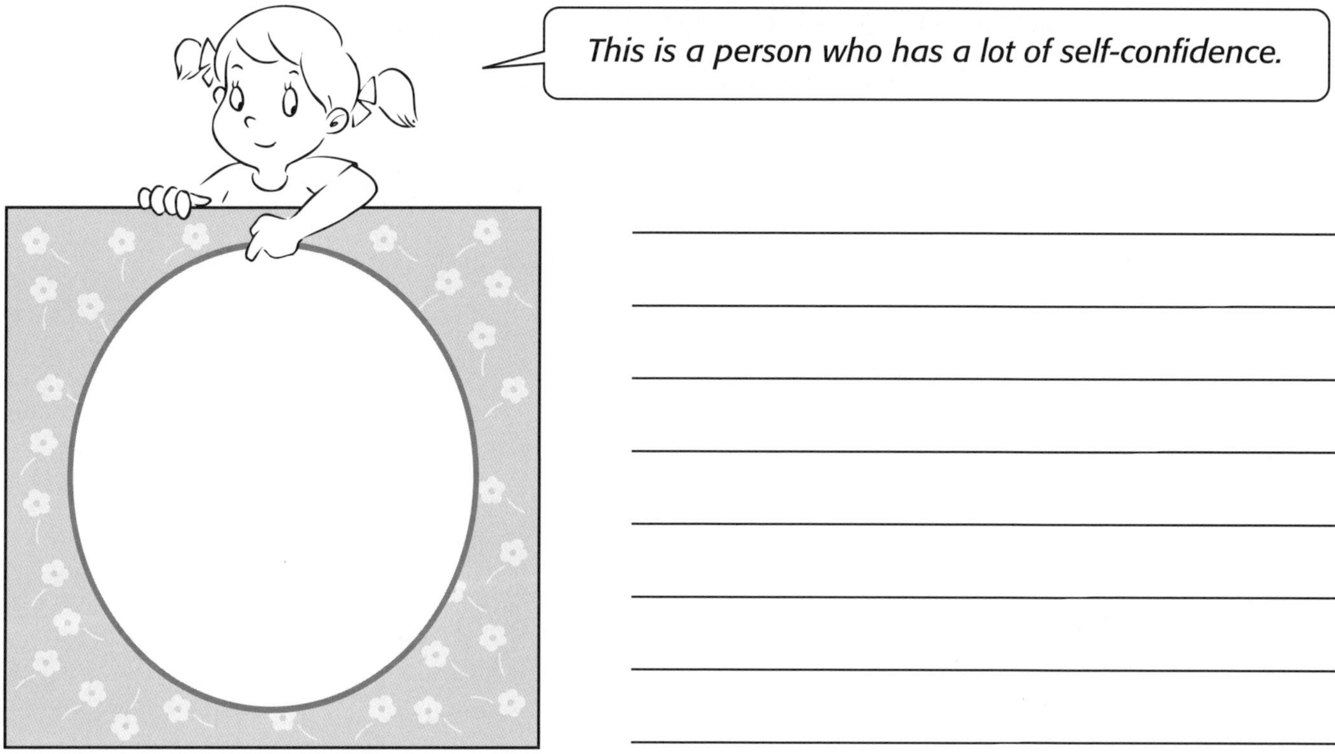

Explain why you think self-confidence is a desirable trait to have.

Name: Date:

Self-confidence

Put a checkmark beside the actions and thoughts that you think develop self-confidence. Then answer the question.

Actions and Thoughts Needed to Develop Self-confidence

- ❍ Compare your accomplishments with the accomplishments of others.
- ❍ Keep your thoughts and wishes to yourself.
- ❍ Practise speaking in front of others.
- ❍ Compare yourself with others.
- ❍ Do things you enjoy.
- ❍ Envy what others have.
- ❍ Follow your interests.
- ❍ Copy your friends.
- ❍ Respect yourself.
- ❍ Think positively.
- ❍ Be assertive.

Which one do you think is the most important? Why?

Name: Date:

Self-confidence

Read the comic. Answer the questions.

Alice on a Stage

1. Describe something you have done that took self-confidence.

____

____

____

2. What gave you the self-confidence to do this?

____

____

____

3. How did it make you feel afterwards?

____

____

____

Name: Date:

Self-confidence

Fill out the sheet to help you understand yourself better.

Self-confidence comes not from doing things well, but from knowing what our strengths and weaknesses are.

Areas to be considered:

- math
- music
- art
- language
- animals
- patience
- science
- listening
- fixing things
- sports

All about Me

My strengths are:

My weaknesses are:

Areas where I have the most self-confidence:

Areas where I have the least self-confidence:

Name: Date:

Self-confidence

Read the two quotations. Choose the one you like better and explain why. Then describe an experience you've had that fits the quotation.

"Who has confidence in himself will gain the confidence of others."

– Leib Lazarow

"Your chances of success in any undertaking can always be measured by your belief in yourself."

– Robert Collier

I like the quotation by ____________________ better because ____________________

____

____

____

My Own Experience with this Quotation:

____

____

____

____

Name: Date:

Creativity

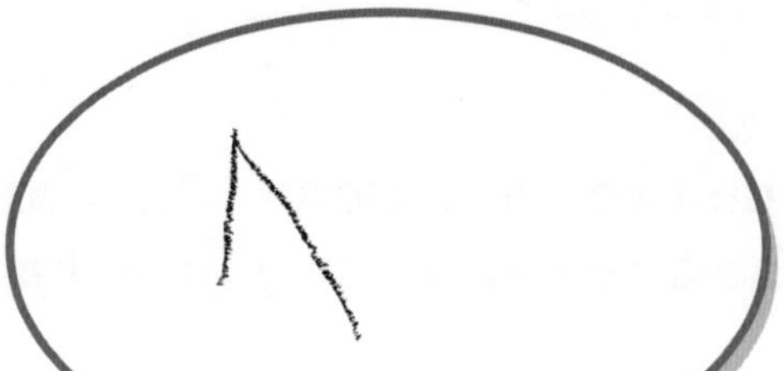

Every Friday, the children in Ms. Cartwright's class take turns drawing on the board. Today it is Nancy's turn. She draws one line down and another down and to the right. Then the bell rings. She drops the chalk and runs out to play.

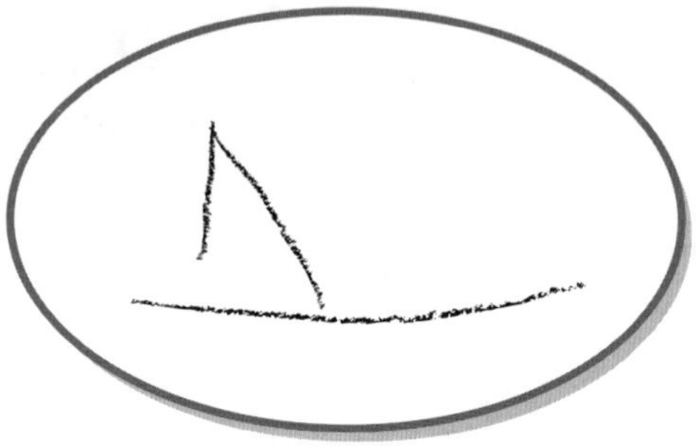

Mackenzie picks up the chalk before she leaves for recess. "I wonder what Nancy was drawing," she thinks. "Oh! It's a whale," she says, and she starts to finish Nancy's picture of a whale – until Marta bumps into her and she drops the chalk, remembers it's recess, and runs out to play.

Marta looks up at the picture Mackenzie was drawing on the board. "It must be a sailboat," she thinks. Marta picks up the chalk and completes the picture. Then she runs out to play.

The bell rings, and the children come in from recess and sit in their seats. Nancy stares at the funny writing on the blackboard. "Great idea!" she says. She jumps up and finishes writing her name on the blackboard.

Creativity is turning the expected into the unexpected. It is making something out of nothing, more out of less, and the wondrous from the ordinary.

Name: Date:

Creativity

Read the problems. Do some creative problem solving. Then write your ideas for creative solutions.

1. The drama club is using the gymnasium all week. Rain is in the forecast all week, too. Your gym teacher needs some creative ideas for keeping her students physically active this week.

2. You've promised to help your dad build a new patio, which will take up every Saturday in the spring. You've also just got a part in the community play and have learned that practice sessions are held on Saturdays. What creative ideas can you come up with that allow you to do both?

Name: Date:

Creativity

Draw an outline of your hand on the page. (You may want to overlap more than one outline.) What else could it be? Turn it into something else, and compare your ideas with those of your classmates.

My Transformed Handprint

Name: Date:

Creativity

Complete the chart. Then cut it out and keep it in an eye-catching place to remind yourself to pursue creativity.

Creative Pursuits

I have tried:

I will continue with:

I would like to try:

Name: Date:

Creativity

Writing Poetry (I)

Read what the children say. Then write your poem on the next page.

Often, rules force us to be more creative than we would be without them. This is true of fixed-form poems, which have rules we follow to create them.

Creativity is not just arts and crafts. It can be a piece of writing.

Try your hand at one of these two forms (or both if you have time), and see where it takes you.

Form I: **Acrostic**

The first letter of each line forms a word or message when read in a sequence.

Form II: **Haiku**

It is a non-rhyming poem about something from the natural world that is sparsely worded and follows a specific format.

Acrostic

Creatures find me wherever I am
Rain or sun, school or home
Elephants in my closet
Antelopes in my lunch box
Tigers sleeping in my bed
Iguanas in my bathtub
Vultures perched on each desk
Every day for me is like a trip to the zoo

Haiku

1st line → 5 syllables

2nd line → 7 syllables

3rd line → 5 syllables

Name: Date:

Creativity

Writing Poetry (II)

Try using the quotations as inspiration for your poetry.

"Another word for creativity is courage."

– George Prince

"Creativity is the ability to see relationships where none exist."

– Thomas Disch

Acrostic

C ______________________________

R ______________________________

E ______________________________

A ______________________________

T ______________________________

I ______________________________

V ______________________________

E ______________________________

Haiku

____

____

____

Name: Date:

Bullying

Bullying is one person taking his or her aggression out on another, less powerful person. We recognize it easily when bullies pick on their targets again and again. But bullying is not always a repeated act; it can be a one-time occurrence if the bully realizes the victim is not as weak as originally thought, or if the bully is only passing through. Whether bullying happens repeatedly or just once, it is hurtful and scary for the person being bullied.

A bully's aggression can be physical: punching or hurting in any other way, or it can be verbal: talking about a person behind his or her back, or saying mean things to him or her.

A person who bullies another is not being brave or funny or smart. A bully targets a younger or smaller person or someone unlikely or unable to fight back. Bullying is always a cowardly act.

Name: Date:

Bullying

What does bullying look like? Identify each kind of bullying. Write your answer in the box. Then choose one kind and describe a similar situation that you were either a part of or witnessed.

taking someone's belongings
physical aggression
social exclusion
spreading rumours

My Experience

Name: Date:

Bullying

Answer the following questions.

1. *Why do you think bullies choose those who are weaker than they are to pick on?*

2. Describe a bullying incident you witnessed.

3. At the time, did you recognize it as bullying? If yes, did you report it to a teacher or other authority?

4. Would you recognize or react to bullying any differently today?

Name: Date:

Bullying

Write "T" for true or "F" for false for each sentence. Rewrite the five false sentences to make them true.

1. Making a person feel stupid is a form of bullying. ________
2. An act of aggression is only bullying if it is repeated over and over. ________
3. Calling names is not bullying. ________
4. Bullies cannot be stopped. ________
5. Fighting a bully with physical aggression is a good way to deal with bullying. ________
6. Not all teasing is bullying. ________
7. Making a person do something he or she doesn't want to do is a form of bullying. ________
8. An argument a sister and a brother have over the largest slice of pie is bullying. ________

Correcting the Five False Sentences:

____

____

____

____

____

Name: Date:

Bullying

Use each of the following words in a sentence about bullying.

aggression

tease

rumour

bullied

witness

Name: Date:

Bullying

Read what Jason says. Choose one of the messages and make it the theme of a poster. Fill out the sheet below so that you know what all of the elements of the poster will be before you start. Then create your polished poster on construction paper.

Not everyone recognizes bullying, even when they are the bullies or they witness bullying. Also, many people don't know what to do if they do witness bullying.

Messages to Be Considered for Themes:

1. Bullying is not courageous; it is cowardly.
2. Tell a trusted adult if you witness bullying or are being bullied.
3. The coolest thing a person can do is care.

Plan for MY POSTER

Title: ______________________

Size and Colour(s): ______________________

Images (of bullying, of friendship, of trusted adults, etc.):

____

Materials (magazine cutouts, pencils, crayons, paint, etc.):

____

Decorations (ribbon, glitter, buttons, stickers):

____

Other Writing I Want to Include:

____

Canadian Character Education Grades 5-6

Project Ideas

Quotations on Character Traits

Materials:

- construction paper
- coloured pencils or markers
- hole punch
- string

What to do:

1. Choose ten character traits.
2. Find one quotation for each of these character traits from the library or the Internet.
3. Write a character trait at the top of each sheet of construction paper as the title.
4. Write the quotation on the sheet.
5. Think of a person who has this character trait. Write about the person and explain how he or she demonstrates the character trait on the following sheet.
6. Repeat steps 3 to 5 for the remaining nine character traits.
7. Think of a title for your book.
8. Design a cover.
9. Punch holes along the left side of all the sheets.
10. Tie the sheets together with string.
11. Choose your favourite quotation and show the page to your classmates. Tell them why you like this quotation best.

My Character Traits

Materials:

- paper
- pencil or ball pen
- transparent tape

Directions:

1. The teacher writes lists of character traits on the board, both good and bad.
2. Each student is given a sheet of paper.
3. Students write "My Character Traits" at the top as the title. Then they draw a line down the middle of the paper. Finally, they write "Good" at the top of the left column and "Bad" for the right column.
4. Students help each other stick the sheets of paper on each other's backs.
5. Students walk around and have others to write their character traits on the sheets – one good and one bad (use words from the lists provided by the teacher).
6. Each student makes sure that every classmate has written on his or her sheet before he or she sees what others think of him or her.
7. Each student draws up a plan for how he or she can improve regarding any bad character traits.

Character Traits

Good	Bad
• honest	• shy
• generous	• passive
• loyal	• disrespectful
• self-disciplined	• unreliable
• patient	• pessimistic
• reliable	• not punctual
• friendly	• careless

Character Traits for a Career

Career Ideas

- firefighter
- actor/actress
- gardener
- professional athlete
- flight attendant
- pizza deliverer
- coach
- accountant
- construction worker
- nanny
- vet
- librarian
- tour guide
- school bus driver

Materials:

- slips of paper
- marker
- old tissue box

Directions:

1. The teacher writes a different career on each slip of paper (enough for the whole class).
2. The slips of paper are folded and put in an old tissue box.
3. Each student draws a slip from the box.
4. The student thinks of what character traits a person of that career should possess and why those character traits are important for the career.
5. The students take turns telling the class their ideas.
6. Other students can add character traits that they think are important for the career when each student has finished his or her presentation.

A school bus driver must have patience. He or she needs patience to resolve conflict, if there is any, among children on the school bus.

Character Traits in a Story

What to Do:

1. Read a story you like.
2. Pay attention to the character traits of the main character.
3. Draw a cover for the book.
4. Complete the activity below.
5. Tell your classmates how the character's traits help him or her solve the problem in the story.

Cover of My Favourite Book

Main Character: ____________________

His / Her Character Traits:

____

____

____

How These Character Traits Help Him / Her Solve the Problem:

____

____

____

____

Character Trait Board Game

What to Do:

1. In groups of four, brainstorm about what the board game will be like and how the game will be played.
2. Design the setting and draw routes on the board. Divide the routes into small spaces with instructions written on them.

   e.g. Think of a word related to "patience".
3. Players may be required to draw from stacks of cards when they land on certain spaces.

   e.g. Good Character Trait Card – You volunteered to help on Save the Earth Day. Go two spaces forward.

   Bad Character Trait Card – You told a lie. Stay where you are for two rounds.
4. Decide on the rules of the game.

   e.g. Whenever a player lands on a space with a character trait written on it, he or she has to think of one way to show that character trait. If the player fails to do so within a time limit, he or she will have to go back one space.
5. Show the game to your classmates and explain the rules.
6. Play the game together and have fun!

Materials:

- a large coloured Bristol board
- coloured pencils or markers
- a stack of small blank cards
- other materials of your choice
- dice
- scissors and glue

Character Trait Acrostic Poem

Materials:

- construction paper
- coloured pencils or markers
- other materials of your choice

Choose a character trait. Write an acrostic poem with the word on the construction paper. Highlight the topic word with colour or design. Then draw pictures to go with your poem and share your poem with your classmates.

Goodies in my snack bag
Riley and Roy, my friends
Apples fresh from the market
TV shows enjoyed with my family
Ice cream shared with my brother
Teachers whom I respect
Usual things in my daily life
Deep from my heart I am thankful for them
Everlasting happiness I then will get!

Use each letter of the word as the first letter of the first word of each line.

Coat of Arms – Page 1

The colour and design on a coat of arms has specific meaning. They symbolize specific character traits or personal values. Review the meanings of colours and common heraldic symbols used in different coats of arms.

Coat of Arms

Colour

- **Or** (Gold)
  Generosity
- **Argent** (Silver or White)
  Sincerity; Peace
- **Purpure** (Purple)
  Justice; Sovereignty; Regal
- **Azure** (Blue)
  Strength; Loyalty
- **Vert** (Green)
  Hope; Loyalty in Love
- **Sable** (Black)
  Constancy; Grief
- **Tenne / Tawny** (Orange)
  Worthwhile Ambition
- **Sanguine / Murray** (Maroon)
  Victory; Patience in Battle
- **Gules** (Red)
  Warrior; Martyr;
  Military Strength

Common Symbols

Feathers
Obedience; Serenity

Heart
Charity; Sincerity

Ivy Leaves
Strong and Lasting Friendship

Flowers
Hope; Joy

Hand
Faith; Sincerity; Justice

Beaver
Industriousness; Perseverance

Dog
Loyalty; Vigilance; Courage

Goose
Resourcefulness

Lion
Courage; Strength

Deer
Peace; Harmony

Arm / Hand in Armour
Leadership

Coat of Arms – Page 2

What to Do:

1. Pick a classmate and think of specific character traits he or she demonstrates.
2. Design a coat of arms for him or her, using the colours and symbols that represent his or her specific character traits.
3. Cut out the coat of arms and give it to your classmate.

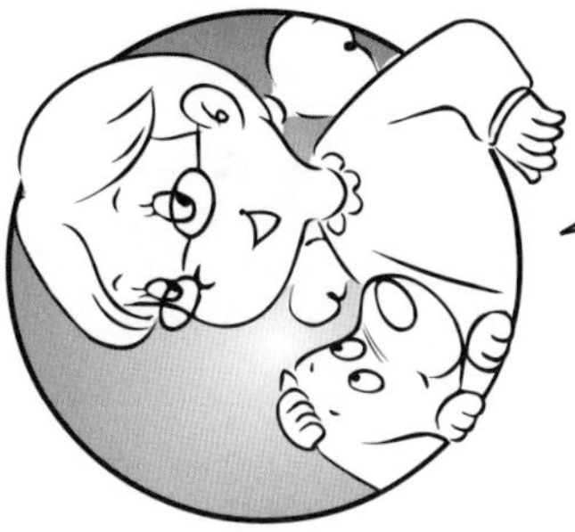

You may find more information about heraldic symbols and their meanings in the library or on the Internet.